CW00602196

PENGUIN BOO

Action Replay

Anecdotal Poems edited by Michael Rosen

STOCKTON BOROUGH

WITHDRAWN

LIBRARIES

0026172119

0026172119

By the same author

CULTURE SHOCK

Action Replay

Anecdotal Poems edited by
Michael Rosen

Illustrated by Andrzej Krauze

Stockton Borough Public Libraries 5/97

0026172119   808·81

PENGUIN BOOKS

PENGUIN BOOKS

Published by the Penguin Group
Penguin Books Ltd, 27 Wrights Lane, London W8 5TZ, England
Penguin Books USA Inc., 375 Hudson Street, New York, New York 10014, USA
Penguin Books Australia Ltd, Ringwood, Victoria, Australia
Penguin Books Canada Ltd, 10 Alcorn Avenue, Toronto, Ontario, Canada M4V 3B2
Penguin Books (NZ) Ltd, 182–190 Wairau Road, Auckland 10, New Zealand

Penguin Books Ltd, Registered Offices: Harmondsworth, Middlesex, England

First published by Viking, 1993
Published in Penguin Books 1994
1 3 5 7 9 10 8 6 4 2

This selection copyright © Michael Rosen, 1993
Illustrations copyright © Andrzej Krauze, 1993
All rights reserved

The Acknowledgements on pages 109 to 119 constitute
an extension of their copyright page

Printed in England by Clays Ltd, St Ives plc
Filmset in Monophoto Sabon

Except in the United States of America, this book is sold subject
to the condition that it shall not, by way of trade or otherwise, be lent,
re-sold, hired out, or otherwise circulated without the publisher's
prior consent in any form of binding or cover other than that in
which it is published and without a similar condition including this
condition being imposed on the subsequent purchaser

Contents

Introduction

This is a collection of anecdotes – short stories that people might have told each other over a meal or on a bus. Perhaps they did, perhaps they didn't, but we do know for certain that they chose to write them down. This was a way of capturing their experiences, of sharing them with a wider audience, an audience they will never know or even see.

Most of them are, I think, accounts of events and happenings in the poets' lives. A few are moments in history that the poets have thought worth telling. The writing comes from all over the world; some of the poets are our contemporaries, while others lived hundreds of years ago.

I hope that at least one thing written here will encourage anyone reading this book to talk, tell stories of their own and (who knows?), try writing something.

Michael Rosen

Halfway Street, Sidcup

'We did sums at school, Mummy –
you do them like this: look.' I showed her.

It turned out she knew already.

Fleur Adcock

Love at First Sight

Their eyes met
when they dropped their contact lenses
into the same bowl of water.

John Agard

I had to get up early last Sunday,
Mum wanted bread from the shop.
It was cold outside, and quiet,
Except for an occasional car.
Five men came towards me,
All dressed in overalls,
Pushing rusty black carts.
The men were black.
I watched them and wondered,
Is this why they came here?
Leaving beautiful islands in the sun
To sweep England's dirty streets?
They looked defeated,
Wearily pushing their carts up the steep hill.
Occasionally they talked,
Mumbling words I could not hear.
I continued my walk,
Wondering.

Sandra Agard

Taking a Visitor to See the Ruins

(for Joe Bruchac)

He's still telling about the time he came west
and was visiting me. I knew he wanted to see
some things, like everybody sees
when they're out in the wilds of New Mexico.
So when we had had our coffee that morning
after he'd arrived I said
would you like to go see some old
Indian ruins?
His eyes brightened with excitement,
he was thinking, no doubt,
of places like he had known.
Mohawk caves filled with falseface masks,
brown skins friendly, long-abandoned
pueblo ruins carved and built into tall
sandstone cliffs, connecting
with the people, with the ancient land.
Sure, he said, I'd like that a lot.
Come on, I said, and we got in my car.
We drove a few blocks to a tall
high-security apartment building,
went up the walk and pressed the buzzer.
They answered and we went upstairs,
past the pool room, past the party room
down the hall, 'Look, that's the outdoor pool,'
I said. We went up five flights
in the elevator, down the hall to knock on the door.
'Joe,' I said, when we'd gotten inside
the chic apartment that overlooked the town,
'I'd like you to meet the old Indian ruins
I promised. My mother, Mrs Francis,
and my grandmother, Mrs Gottlieb.'

His eyes grew large, and then he laughed,
looking shocked at the two grinning faces
of the women he'd just met. They laughed too.
And he's still telling the tale of the old
Indian ruins he visited in New Mexico
who are still living pueblo style
up high where the enemy can't reach them,
just like in the olden times.

Paula Gunn Allen

Dad said that at
least my rotten
marks at school
prove that I
haven't been cheating.

Anon.

Real Life

It was a hot day thrown suddenly cool
By that hard rain, poured off the slate-roof barn
When the boy was hit by lightning.
Standing safe, he thought, in the large doorway,
Eaves above him tapping,
Farm trucks shining up.
Big for his age, father's overalls, watching things,
Whole complexion tan like pure maple syrup,
The stuff he gathered with his grandfather and horses.
His old man and older brothers stoke and boil the
    woodfire,
Spend those long nights in the sugar house.
The way the light spills out of the small steamy windows
All over the snow, dreamy in the valley.

Well a mean bolt came down from the sky to end that,
A splitting axe flying.
Water dripping smooth from the roof edge
Splashes on to his boots and cuffs,
Hayseed still itching his back,
Cows poking behind him in their stalls,
Need a light already it's getting so dark, he thought –
Struck him from the forehead straight down,
Cracked him open like nothing should be.
The family dog lay nearby on a broken bale
Like he has for 15 Julys,
His large head on his paws, tilted and watching
Rain burning the ground.

Bob Arnold

seven

with seven-year-old strength
i tried
to pull him
back
but he hit her
with a closed fist
anyway
and she yelled and yelled
and said
        what will the neighbours think?

Astra

13 and 625 Lines

They made a row of us on the sofa,
ten, ten, seven and five –
they turned off the TV.
Daddy was crying so we cried too,
though I didn't know why, exactly.

My sister put the TV back on
and we all watched *Tom and Jerry*
without laughing.

The house was sold
and they argued quietly about possessions.
Dad said
If Mum is having you lot
then I'm bloody well having the photo albums.

Ros Barber

I feel exhausted!
When I woke up
this morning both
my eyes were
still open!

Anon.

Changing the Wheel

I sit on the roadside bank.
The driver changes a wheel.
I do not like the place I have come from.
I do not like the place I am going to.
Why do I watch him changing the wheel
With impatience?

Bertolt Brecht

*(trans. from the German by Michael Hamburger
and Christopher Middleton)*

Road

They tore up the old road
and buried it under a new one.
I didn't mind

Pete Brown

A Friend of the Indians

A man who was known
as a friend of the Indians
spoke to Red Jacket one day
about the good treatment
the Senecas enjoyed
from their white neighbors.

Red Jacket walked with him
beside the river, then suggested
they should sit together
on a log next to the stream.

They both sat down.
Then Red Jacket slid closer
to the man and said, 'Move Over.'

The man moved over, but when he did
Red Jacket again slid closer.
'Move Over,' he said.

Three times this happened
until the man had reached
the end of the log near the water.
Then, once more, he was told, 'Move Over.'

'But if I move further
I shall fall in the water,'
the man pleaded,
teetering on the edge.

Red Jacket replied,
'And even so you whites
tell us to move on when
no place is left to go.'

Joseph Bruchac

coffee

I was having a coffee at the
counter
when a man
3 or 4 stools down
asked me,
'listen, weren't you the
guy who was
hanging from his
heels
from that 4th floor
hotel room
the other
night?'

'yes,' I answered, 'that
was me.'

'what made you do
that?' he asked.

'well, it's pretty
involved.'

he looked away
then.

the waitress
who had been
standing there
asked me,
'he was joking,
wasn't
he?'

'no,' I
said.

I paid, got up, walked
to the door, opened
it.

I hear the man
say, 'that guy's
nuts.'

out on the street I
walked north
feeling
curiously
honored.

Charles Bukowski

education

at that small inkwell desk
I had trouble with the words
'sing' and 'sign'.
I don't know why
but
'sing' and 'sign':
it bothered
me.

the others went on and learned
new things
but I just sat there
thinking about
'sing' and 'sign'.
there was something there
I couldn't
overcome.

what it gave me was a
bellyache as
I looked at the backs of all those
heads.

the lady teacher had a
very fierce face
it ran sharply to a
point
and was heavy with white
powder.

one afternoon
she asked my mother to come
see her
and I sat with them
in the classroom
as they
talked.

'he's not learning
anything,' the teacher
told my
mother.

'please give him a
chance, Mrs Sims!'

'he's not *trying*, Mrs
Chinaski!'

my mother began to cry.

Mrs Sims sat there
and watched
her.

it went on for some
minutes.

then Mrs Sims said,
'well, we'll see what we
can do . . .'

then I was walking with
my mother
we were walking in
front of the school,
there was much green grass
and then the
sidewalk.

'oh Henry,' my mother said,
'your father is so disappointed in
you, I don't know what we are
going to do!'

father, my mind said,
father and father and
father.

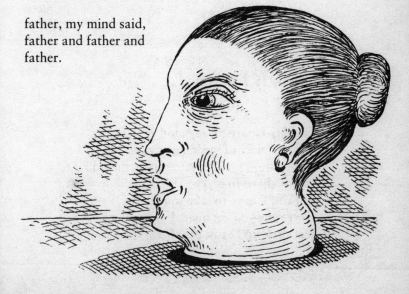

words like that.

I decided not to learn anything
in that
school.

my mother walked along
beside me.
she wasn't anything at
all.
and I had a bellyache
and even the trees we walked
under
seemed less than
trees
and more like everything
else.

Charles Bukowski

The Day I Married . . .

The day I married, my mother
had one piece of wedding advice:
'Don't make good potato salad,' she told me,
'it's too hard to make
and you'll have to take something
every time you get invited somewhere.
Just cook up beans, people eat them too.'

My mother was good at potato salad
and part of the memories of my childhood
have to do with endless batches made
for family get-togethers, church picnics,
Civitan suppers, Democratic party fund raisers,
whatever event called for potato salad.

I'd peel the hard-boiled eggs.
My mother would pack her big red plastic picnic bowl
high with yellow potato salad (she used mustard)
and it would sit proud on endless tables
and come home empty.

What my mother might and could have said
is choose carefully what you get good at
cause you'll spend the rest of your life
doing it. But I didn't hear that.
I was young and anxious to please
and I knew her potato salad secrets.

And the thousand other duties
given to daughters by mothers
and sometimes I envy those women
who get by with pots of beans.

Jo Carson

Picture from the Blitz

After all these years
I can still close my eyes and see
her sitting there,
in her big armchair,
grotesque under an open sky,
framed by the jagged lines of her broken house.

Sitting there,
a plump homely person,
steel needles still in her work-rough hands;
grey with dust, stiff with shock,
but breathing,
no blood or distorted limbs;
breathing, but stiff with shock,
knitting unravelling on her apron'd knee.

They have taken the stretchers off my car
and I am running
under the pattering flak
over a mangled garden;
treading on something soft
and fighting the rising nausea –
only a far-flung cushion, bleeding feathers.

They lift her gently
out of her great armchair,
tenderly,
under the open sky,
a shock-frozen woman trailing khaki wool.

Lois Clark

One night in 1940
My father lost my mum
He came home from the pub one night
And found that she had gone
I'd gone off to the country
And came back after a week
She'd gone off with a docker –
What a bleedin' cheek!
And if anyone asked my father
What had happened to my mum
He'd sadly say he'd lost her –
And they assumed she'd been blown up by a bomb

Dan Colman

A Recollection

My father's friend came once to tea.
He laughed and talked. He spoke to me.
But in another week they said
That friendly pink-faced man was dead.

'How sad . . .' they said, 'the best of men . . .'
So I said too, 'How sad'; but then
Deep in my heart I thought, with pride,
'I know a person who has died.'

Frances Cornford

'right here the other night something
odd occurred' charlie confessed
(halting) 'a tall strong young
finelooking fellow, dressed

well but not over, stopped
me by "could you spare three cents please"
– why guess who nearly leaped
out of muchtheworseforwear shoes

"fair friend" we enlightened this stranger
"some people have all the luck;
since our hero is quite without change, you're
going to get one whole buck"

not a word this stranger replied –
but as one whole buck became his
(believe it or don't) by god
down this stranger went on both knees'

green turns red (the roar
of traffic collapses: through
west ninth slowly cars pour
into sixth avenue)

'then; my voice marvels 'what happened'
as everywhere red goes green
– groping blank sky with a blind
stare, he whispers 'i ran'

e.e. cummings

Fire Down Below

Utterly
Without warning
Overnight
My father's thick black hair
Turned white.
With anxious tears in her eyes
My mother viewed him
With surprise and consternation.
'Your hair has turned as white as snow.'
Placatingly he said, 'I know.'
'And yet, my dear,
There is no proof
That when the snow
Is on the roof
The fire has gone out
In the boiler.'

Ginnie Lewis Digham

Sexism in 1972

I said to Ann
the woman I was living with
I always wanted to be a woman
I would have done more or less the same things
but I would have had more fun doing them
but she said
What makes you think you'd have been able
to do them??
I didn't have an answer to that

Jas H. Duke

'I just saw a tomato squashed in the road – oh God, it
could have been a person!'

Overheard at an American lunch counter

Happy Mothers Day

In a drunken stupor
My mother said to me,
'You should have been stillborn.'
Thank you, Mum,
Now I understand
The meaning of true love,
The cord has been cut,
Years of anguish erased,
And now I shall never
Have to see you again.

Sharon Dunham

I nearly died

In the pub
I was feeling gloomy
for I was
being drafted
into the army.

'It won't be so bad,'
my mate said.
'All you've got to do
is to make them laugh.'
Laugh? I nearly died!

Bill Eburn

The Trust

In a small town
        in a school
a boy caught a tired butterfly
and as she tried to get free
the purple-blue of her wings
was powdered into the air
The boy put her
on a table, under a paperweight
he burned her wings with matches
he cut her corpse
in half
with his penknife

That boy has gone, but
for thirty years
I've had his dirty penknife
and on the penknife
those brownish-yellow bloodstains
trouble me –
an acid taste on my tongue
a tense fatigue
        I'm bone-weary
        but I can't sleep

Saqi Farooqi

(*trans. from the Urdu by Frances W. Pritchett*)

35

Programme cover

I slap down 50p
For an Ipswich Town programme.
I gaze at the cover
For a couple of seconds,
And to my amazement
I see my own printed face
Staring up at me
In front of the crowd.
I remember,
It was hot,
It was August,
Town v. the Owls.
The roar ravaged my ears.
The first game of the season.
There, on the programme,
My brother sits upright,
Biting his fingernails
With excitement and hope.
And me?
I am looking anxious,
Apprehensive,
Knowing my team
Is going to lose.

Evelyne Freeman (14)

Four Years

The smell of him went soon
From all his shirts.
I sent them for jumble,
And the sweaters and suits.
The shoes
Held more of him; he was printed
Into his shoes. I did not burn
Or throw or give them away.
Time has denatured them now.

Nothing left.
There never will be
A hair of his in a comb.
But I want to believe
That in the shifting of housedust
Minute presences still drift:
An eyelash,
A hard crescent cut from a fingernail,
That sometimes
Between the folds of a curtain
Or the covers of a book
I touch
A flake of his skin.

Pamela Gillilan

Family Matters

In our museum – we always go there on Sundays –
they have opened a new department.
Our aborted children, pale, serious embryos,
sit there in plain glass jars
and worry about their parents' future.

Günter Grass

(*trans. from the German by Michael Hamburger
and Christopher Middleton*)

Just Waiting

Waiting. Down by the Town Hall.
Waiting. Some laughing,
some talking, some squatting,
some just posing.
All waiting. Just waiting.
Outside the Library
waiting for someone
or something or nothing.
At the Tube Station
phoning, taking photos
in the booth, queuing
and waiting.
During the day
shopping, rushing, banking,
pushing, chatting, eating,
then waiting.

Maybe for a bus
or a loved one
or the strike of the clock
telling them it's time
to move on to another spot
to wait.
A young man stood
and looked around himself.
It was a sunny day
and it was pleasant to
take in the sun, the air
and the scenes as he waited.
It was his day off.
He was determined
to do nothing to exert himself
so here he was outside
the pub where he never drank.
A copper came up to him.
'What are you waiting for, son?'
'Nothing,' he replied.
'Well move along then.'
He didn't want to cause trouble
so he simply set off
to find another spot to gaze.
After all he knew that since the riots
Babylon were just waiting.

Monique Griffiths

Tribal Cemetery

I lay my hand
Upon
The coldness of the smooth
White stone,
My fingers touch the words,
I read again:
My father's name,
Date of birth,
Date of death,
Veteran of
World War I.

'This is your
Grandfather's grave,'
I tell my children,
Wishing I could tell them,
That they would understand,
That the man
Who was my father
Was of that first generation,
Born on old land
Newly made reservation,
That at twelve,
He went to Mission School,
To learn to wear shoes,
To eat with knife and fork,
To pray to the Catholic God,
To painfully
Learn English words,
English meanings,
White ways of thinking,
English words,

To speak,
To think,
To write,
English words,
When we,
My children
And I,
Know no others.

I lay my hand
Upon
The cold white
Stone,
My daughter,
Who is four,
Gathers small rocks,
With which she
Fills her pockets,
She sings to herself
As she goes along.

My son,
Who is ten,
Stays with me a while,
Beside my father's grave,
Asks me about my
Childhood,
About the others,
Lying buried here,
In Campbell-labelled
graves.
Then he leaves me,
And goes about
The cemetery,
Reading tombstones

For unusual names,
Looking for people
Who lived
One hundred years,
Or more –
He's found five.

Janet Campbell Hale

Well, it's Today Already

Well, it's today already.

I don't know how it got here,
but there's a funny echo in this room.   room

Martin Hall

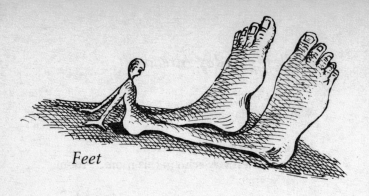

Feet

I was made aware of my feet today
In a quite unusual way.
A lady wanted to massage them for me.
Hesitantly I put my feet in her lap,
One at a time,
And she kneaded them
Like stiff Plasticine.

Feet are more sensitive
Than I ever gave them credit for,
And I felt bad that I'd neglected
Their finer feelings
For so long.

The hands that took my feet
Were warm.
Not cold and professional
Or hot and erotic
But warm.
And I came away feeling
How nice to be touched,
To make contact,
Even through your feet.

Mark Haviland

Morning Poem
(for Deirdre)

'I've just about reached
breaking point'
he snapped.

    Adrian Henri

The Steam Car

When Josef Bozek, the inventor,
constructed his steam-driven
car, followed by his
steam-driven 'water boat',
seven yards long,
he organized, 1 June 1817,
a public showing in Stromovka Park
for the high nobility
and the enlightened public
upon payment of an entrance fee.

Things had no sooner begun
than there was a sudden downpour
and in the resulting confusion
somebody stole the cash box
and the proceeds.

So that Bozek, the inventor,
lost all his money.

He demolished the steam car
with a sledge-hammer.

Since that time
no steam-driven conveyances
have been seen in Bohemia.

The downpours
come frequently.

Miroslav Holub

(*trans. from the Czech by David Young
and Dana Hábora*)

A War Film

I saw,
With a catch of the breath and the heart's uplifting,
Sorrow and pride,
   The 'week's great draw' –
The Mons Retreat;
The 'Old Contemptibles' who fought, and died,
The horror and the anguish and the glory.

As in a dream,
Still hearing machine-guns rattle and shells scream,
I came out into the street.

When the day was done,
My little son
Wondered at bath-time why I kissed him so,
Naked upon my knee.
How could he know
The sudden terror that assaulted me? . . .
The body I had borne
Nine moons beneath my heart,
A part of me . . .
If, someday,
It should be taken away
To War. Tortured. Torn.
Slain.
Rotting in No Man's Land, out in the rain –
My little son . . .
Yet all those men had mothers, every one.

How should he know
Why I kissed and kissed and kissed him, crooning his
   name?
He thought that I was daft.
He thought it was a game,
And laughed, and laughed.

Teresa Hooley

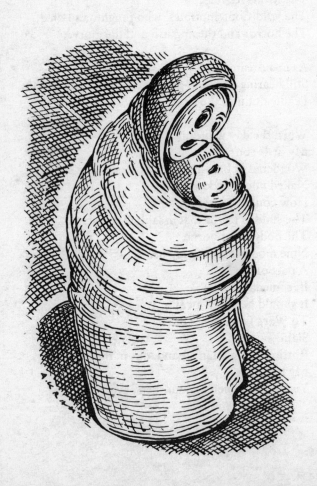

The Changing Face of an Actress

After curtain calls
Her
       face
              falls
– Then someone says Darling
You were marvellous
– and she picks it up again!

Michael Horovitz

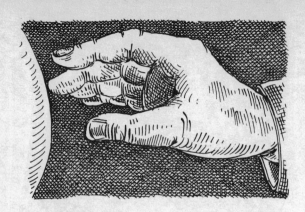

Pants For True

We had spent the day together

That evening
I had on my colorful, sophisticated
        African drummer pants
a soft black belt
pulling in my waist
giving the difference with my hips
a deadly edge

Talk, communication continued
He told me,
'You're what I've been waiting for'
we looking the questions
into each other's eyes

'Touch me,' I said

It wasn't true.

Gloria T. Hull

The Australian Mongrel

Melissa has a dog in her 'in-tray'.
One day she showed me how it worked:
its ears prop up/or
stick out sideways
you can curl them inwards
& make the tail look funny . . .
except it didn't bend as good
as when she first got it
because the wires had broken inside.
I asked her if I could play with it
& its head dropped down on the desk
& its tail drooped
& its ears hung down sadly . . .
finally it collapsed at the knees.
'It's been working like a dog!' I said
& Melissa laughed and I was glad
        she laughed
because of what Don had done.
Don'd come up earlier
& grabbed the dog by the neck.
He made a leash from a Public Service
        Office ribbon
& proceeded to drag the dog along
        the ground:
'Look!'
'The Australian Mongrel'
'Look!!!' & kicked it hard.
& 'Look!' & kicked it again,
& Melissa yelled: 'Don't kick that
        dog!'
& went red in the face because of
        what she'd said

(as if it was 'real' –
a wire-and-plastic toy dog . . .)
but Don didn't hear her anyway.
He showed the whole office – dragging
& kicking the dog
& picking it up
& throwing it hard, head first
    against the sides of people's
    desks.
When he put the dog back (ribbon & all)
he didn't even look at Melissa:
so proud of having made the office laugh
so proud of having made a joke.

Jeltje

The guy
next to me
is doing
Physics
I'm supposed to
be
doing
Chem
But it doesn't
turn
me
on
But then
neither
does
the guy
next
to me

Jenny Kentish

I never got what I wanted.
I always got what I did not want.
What I want
      I shall not get.

Therefore, to get it
      I must not want it
since I get only what I don't want.

      what I want, I can't get
      what I get, I don't want

    I can't get it
because I want it
    I get it
because I don't want it.

I want what I can't get
because
      what I can't get *is* what I want

I don't want what I can get
because
      what I can get *is* what I don't want

I never get what I want
I never want what I get

I get what I deserve
I deserve what I get.

I have it,
      therefore I deserve it

I deserve it
   because I have it.

You have not got it
   therefore you do not deserve it

You do not deserve it
   because you have not got it
You have not got it
   because you do not deserve it

You do not deserve it
therefore you have not got it.

R. D. Laing

I was shopping in Woolworth's when two young assist-
ants passed me on their way upstairs for their tea break.
One said to the other:

   'Well, why don't you like blokes wiv 'airy ear'oles
then?'

Mrs Laura Leggatti

Parents

Linda failed to return home from a dance Friday night.
On Saturday
she admitted she had spent the night
with an Air Force lieutenant.

The Aults decided on a punishment
that would 'wake Linda up'.
They ordered her
to shoot the dog
she had owned about two years.

On Sunday,
the Aults and
Linda
took the dog into the desert
near their home.
They
had the girl
dig a shallow grave.
Then
Mrs Ault
grasped the dog between her hands and
Mr Ault
gave
his daughter
a ·22 caliber pistol
and told her
to shoot the dog.

Stockton Borough
Public Library

Instead,
the girl
put the pistol
to her right temple
and shot herself.

The police said
there were no charges
that could be filed
against the parents
except possibly

cruelty
to
animals.

Julius Lester

Roman Holiday

In Rome, the only summer
we holidayed together,
at a table on the pavement
staring at the Pantheon,
you said that you were

sick of paintings
sick of me
and sick of bloody Italy.
We took a taxi back to the hotel
and I thanked St Peter you were paying.

You spent the next three days
buried in our room.
When at last we stepped on to the train
you managed to smile
and, offering an end to our vendetta,
told me I'd write about this one day.

I remember saying
there are some things
you don't write about.

Tony Lewis-Jones

Daniel at Breakfast

His paper propped against the electric toaster
   (Nicely adjusted to his morning use),
Daniel at breakfast studies world disaster
   And sips his orange juice.

The words dismay him. Headlines shrilly chatter
   Of famine, storm, death, pestilence, decay.
Daniel is gloomy, reaching for the butter.
   He shudders at the way

War stalks the planet still, and men know hunger,
   Go shelterless, betrayed, may perish soon.
The coffee's weak again. In sudden anger
   Daniel throws down his spoon

And broods a moment on the kitchen faucet
   The plumber mended, but has mended ill;
Recalls tomorrow means a dental visit,
   Laments the grocery bill.

Then, having shifted from his human shoulder
   The universal woe, he drains his cup,
Rebukes the weather (surely turning colder),
   Crumples his napkin up
And, kissing his wife abruptly at the door,
Stamps fiercely off to catch the 8:04.

Phyllis McGinley

Overheard in a hospital examination cubicle:

DOCTOR   Now, Mrs Jones, bend the knee please.
MRS JONES   Which way, doctor?

J. M. McKenzie

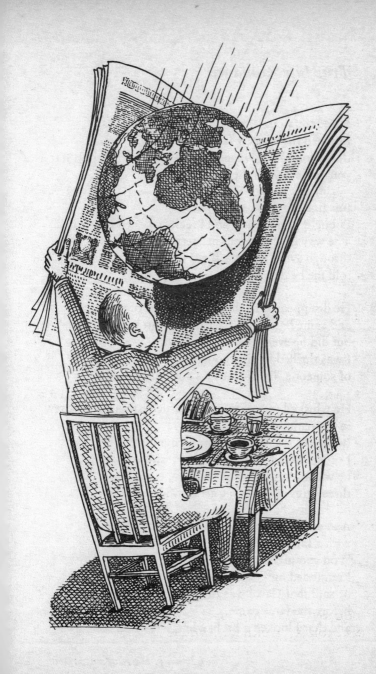

True Life Romance

I used to fall in love with pop stars
I pinned their lovely faces to my wall,
then I found out when you've slept with one pop star
you've slept with them all.

Imagine the après-gig glow,
I bought him a drink and I really enjoyed the show.
The way he thundered masterfully
through every ripped-off riff he knew
told me he'd been practising for years.

He disappeared to the toilets several times
and came back with the early symptoms of a cold –
but did he ever offer me any? No.
I was thrilled by the thought of being on the arm
of someone slightly famous and very drunk.

He whisked me off to a quiet little restaurant he knew
in Tottenham Court Road
(where he was sure he'd be recognized)
I ordered the best doner kebab, with trimmings,
he wasn't hungry so he had
three litres of Kolossi Castle wine to take away.

And as he lurched towards the door
with a far-away look on his face he said:
'You comin' then Carol?'
I reminded him that Carol was not my name
he said that Carol was the name of his first love
before the fame came
and that I looked a bit like her.

All night at the movies,
it was *Ghostbusters* all night.
His lips brushed my ear,
I felt the moist delight of an old belch
and those three little words –
'Pass the wine.'

We watched the dawn rise over King's Cross
and went to his room without view.
He invited me in for a breakfast drink
and (if he was up to it)
a screw.

My head reeled, my heart beat quick and fast
was he to be my first pop star or my last?

Would my name be the refrain in a love song of passion
    and pain?
Would this night be the start of a permanent place in his
    heart?
Would I be able to go on the road with him,
split up after five stormy years and sell my memoirs to a
    Sunday rag?
Would he launch a charity appeal,
be knighted, marry me in a fit of respectability
and settle down in a country mansion
while I presented a weekly pop programme, wearing a
    designer frock?

Probably no. So I went home.

Lindsay MacRae

I went to my uncles wedding
but I got sick so I don't suppose
he'll ask me to his next
one

Mario (6)

Classroom

Teacher talking
writing on the blackboard
students yawning
students talking
'Did you hear about . . .
Tony's had his hair cut . . .
Can you understand this work . . .
They won by seven . . .
Can I borrow . . .
Did you play . . .
That wasn't there before
he went for it'

Noise gets louder
Talking faster

SHUT UP

silence.

Tania Mead

Wednesday Chronicle

On Wednesday I fed the children
and dogs, consulted the almanac
on the time to plant cabbages
cleaned out the kitchen cabinets

A little damp

On Wednesday I fed the children
and dogs, cut my toenails and
observed that they were growing hard
I sneezed a lot

It threatened rain

On Wednesday I fed the children
and dogs, read the newspaper
deplored the state of the nation
and took my pills

An intermittent drizzle

On Wednesday I fed the children
and dogs. In the sink the dishes
teetered. My hands were hot

Rain . . . steady

On Wednesday I fed the children
and dogs and went to bed quite ill

Outside, a thunderstorm

On Wednesday
Skies clear
Consuming blue.

Pamela Mordecai

My lover capable of terrible lies
at night lay close to me
in a dream
that lied like truth.

I woke up, still deceived,
and caressed the bed
thinking it my lover.

It's terrible. I grow lean
in loneliness,
like a water-lily
gnawed by a beetle.

Kaccipēṭṭu Naṉṉākaiyār

(*trans. from the Tamil by A. K. Ramanujan*)

Alcazar

I think I've seen you somewhere,
said the girl in the pub, sitting
at the next table. We joined her,
but could not think where
we might have been together.

At the same table, the fat woman
(happy or sad) said, I wish
I was a bird, I'd take my suitcase
in my beak and fly away
to Copenhagen. Copenhagen?

But that girl in the pub: she was plump,
not smart. She sat
with her husband, married
after a 9-day knowledge of him,
English sailor, ship-jumper.

I'm flying to Copenhagen,
the fat woman said; her suitcase
was not in her beak. The girl and I
could not think where we might have been
together. The beer mounted in us.

The fat woman dreamed. The sailor
complained of the beer and cigarettes here;
the girl spoke of her marriage
and husband. It would be all right, she said,
if he wouldn't burn me with cigarettes.

John Newlove

Varicose Story

I told them their cement floor turned my legs blue!
– that is what the doctor told me.
The blue strings of pain
and the red drips in my calves
throbbed at the day's end.
They had to cut the drumstick open
and clean the tubes with brushes.
The bill came. They wanted five hundred.
We couldn't pay.
I went to the foreman, and told him their
cement floor turned my legs blue!
– What about some compensation?
The foreman asked the boss,
who asked the company doctor,
who asked: 'How do you know it is the floor?'
'Do varicose veins run in the family?'
I don't know. And the boss says:
'We need the cement floor to wash the blood away'
The foreman takes me aside:
'We don't like troublemakers!'
I go to the union. He says:
'Why didn't you come and see us *before*
the operation?'
Why weren't you warning us about the floor and
doing something about it before now?
They send a legal man to the boss.
The company offers one hundred and the union accepts.
We sold the car.
Now everyone exercises their legs.

Caterina Passoni

Unemployed

he gets on the train
at 125th street
and st nickalaus avenue
white shirt black tie
gray suit shoes shine
new york times help
wanted ads under his arm
his hair is neatly
process his wristwatch
does not function
the diamondless ring
he wears cost five dollars
on the block after
all the stores
close down for the day
on the train he takes
out his wallet & counts

500 imaginary dollars
after 59th street
came 42nd street and 8th avenue
& he gets out the train
& walks to the nearest
vending machine
& deposits a nickle
for a pack of dentine
& stares into the broken mirror
of the vending machine
for the next fifteen minutes
assuring himself
that he is looking good
and then he proceeds
to the employment
agencies and five
hours and three
hot dogs and two
hamburgers one pack
of cigarettes
and one pint of wine later
he is still jobless

Piedro Pietri

Drag Act

Ralph West, my hall of residence, held
a beauty show for men in women's clothes,
enjoyed by all except one student who
complained that they were dressed, for he'd seen acts
in Paris wearing only Sellotape.

The subtler types with mousy curls, eye-gloss
and tights took all the first places. The ones
with melons up their sweaters just got laughs.
A skirted slob with a black beard came last –
like some old pirate in a dead girl's clothes.

Later, that fatso, back in macho guise,
ascended to a women's floor – the men
were odd, while we were even – knocked my door
and asked to borrow coffee. Naïvely, I went
to get the jar. He pushed me on the bed.
I hadn't noticed him before he donned
falsies and skirt. I didn't know his name.
Strangely, he looked more female in his clothes –
a flabby-breasted, breathless bearded lady,
trying, pathetically, to prove himself a man,
feeling the need on that night to seem
threatening to someone, not just a laugh.

I threw him off and got him to the door.
As men will do, he tried to shift the blame,
saying, 'You looked as if you wanted it.'

Fiona Pitt-Kethley

Pain

My son was delirious; his eyes were burning
like red krishnachura.* I took his small hands
and held them gently; when I touched his forehead
it was burning with fever. He was panting softly
and his head ached furiously. His small dry lips
were moving gently like a swallow's breast. Outside
the storm raged, beating with fury against the windows.
I shivered and wondered if I should call the doctor again.

Red krishnachuras looked into my eyes. Are you
    suffering
my child? I whispered: try to sleep. I touched his brow.
There was no sound. Only a cat yawned in a distant
    corner
of the room. Sleepless, I wondered if dawn would ever
return, I wondered if I could share his suffering.
And then I realized that when it comes to pain
we are all lonely.

Shamsur Rahman

(*trans. from the Bengali by Pritish Nandy*)

* red flowers

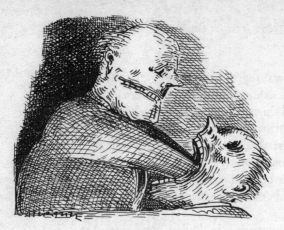

To the Heart

I saw
a cook a specialist
he would put his hand
into the mouth
and through the trachea
push it to the inside
of a sheep
and there in the quick
would grasp the heart
tighten his grip
on the heart
rip out the heart
in one jerk
yes
that was a specialist

Tadeusz Różewicz

(*trans. from the Polish by Czeslaw Milosz*)

'I don't believe this'

I don't believe this;
I've done it again.
But how? I was so careful.
I only used it when I needed to
And sometimes I even went without,
Surely there's some mistake?
But no, I've read it over and over again,
They're right, I know deep down that they are.

What shall I do now?
I'll have to go home, break the news,
Tell him before they do,
They'll be writing it now.
I'll tell him after dinner, he'll be in a good mood
    then,
Perhaps he'll help me out,
He has to, after all if I can't handle it
The responsibility falls on him.
It will be all right, we'll manage
Of course we will,
I mean it's not the first time I've been overdrawn.

E. Russell

Implications

When the charge of election bribery was brought against an Illinois senator, he replied, 'I read the Bible and believe it from cover to cover.'

When his accusers specified five hundred dollars of corruption money was paid in a St Louis hotel bathroom, his friends answered, 'He is faithful to his wife and always kind to his children.'

When he was ousted from the national senate and the doors of his bank were closed by government receivers and a grand jury indicted him, he took the vows of an old established church.

When a jury acquitted him of guilt as a bank wrecker, following the testimony of prominent citizens that he was an honest man, he issued a statement to the public for the newspapers, proclaiming he knew beforehand no jury would darken the future of an honest man with an unjust verdict.

Carl Sandburg

They Carried Their Truth to the Ditch Where They Were Thrown

I'm chatting with Pedro
on the patio of my house
'The harvest's going to be good,' he tells me, and grasping
   some leaves,
he rubs them between his hands, smelling them
   thoughtfully.
Pedro came here today to install the plumbing –
Pedro, whose own house is of cane and clay
      and has no plumbing, the bathroom of the house
      the mountainside around it –
Pedro, who has never had steady work
and merely follows a rut from here to there
and whose partner Luisa has had ten children with
   him . . .
      she told him this morning
      that she's pregnant again.
'Six of our children have died on us,' he tells me.
'The last two were already good strong boys
and helped around the house, serving meals.
The first was Julio, who went at fourteen years old.
The Guard picked him up in the September uprising.
Teodoro (his friend who got away) told me
they put out Julio's eyes so he wouldn't see who tortured
   him
and he followed them, blind and spitting, and a corporal
tossed the eyes to the dogs, and the dogs ate them . . .'
Pedro bows his head (he leans against the lemon tree,
breathes heavily) and then looks up again and goes on:
'Juan, my oldest son, was taken in our neighborhood
and tied so one arm and both legs were broken in front of

all the neighbors
"You son of a big whore," they called him,
"if you're going to open your mouth it better be to
    pray"
       and *wham, wham, wham*
they slammed him in the chest with their gun butts
    until he vomited blood.'
Pedro throws down the spray of lemon blossom,
and the grasshoppers fly up, startled,
and with a hoarse voice, he finishes telling me:
'Those boys of mine said nothing.
They carried their truth to the ditch where they were
    thrown.'

Christian Santos

*(trans. from the Spanish by Anna Kirwan Vogel
and Isabella Halsted)*

Decorated

I watched a jostling mob that surged and yelled,
And fought along the street to see their man:
Was it some drunken bully that they held
For justice – some poor thief who snatched and ran?

I asked a grinning news-boy, 'What's the fun?'
'The beggar did for five of 'em!' said he.
'But if he killed them why's he let off free?'
I queried – 'Most chaps swing for murdering *one*.'
He screamed for joy; and told me, when he'd done –
'It's Corporal Stubbs, the Birmingham VC!'

Siegfried Sassoon

The Cashmere Shawl

It's a long time since lilies of the valley
grew in the Kralupy woods,
as they did in my boyhood,
when I fell in love
with my mother's youngest sister.
She was a few years older than me
and she was beautiful.
Everyone said so.

I knew so little about women then,
and yet my thoughts ceaselessly
revolved round womanhood.
She'd move around me
with just a quiet smile
but never looked me in the eyes
which were burning
as my blood silently exploded
in my veins.

The times I flung my arms wide open
to embrace at least the air
through which she had just passed,
carrying her sweet smile with her
to the next room.

Often I daringly longed
to see her naked,
at least in my dreams.
Or at least naked to her waist,
so that my lips, still innocent of such things,
might bend down close
to her rosy shadows.

When sometimes she had hurried off somewhere,
leaving her cashmere shawl
flung over a chair-back,
I'd press it to my face
and inhale its fragrance.

My vacation was over and I was leaving
for Prague again.
In parting she gave me her hand
and I took it carefully in mine
as if it were a delicate orchid bloom

It's a long time since lilies of the valley
grew in the Kralupy woods.
It's a long time!

Jaroslav Seifert

(*trans. from the Czech by Ewald Osers*)

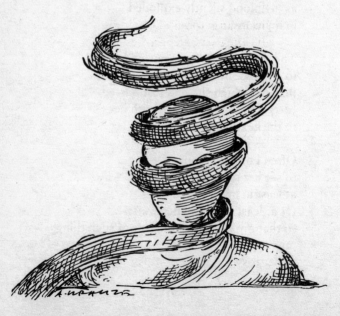

The Pigeon

My father
with a tormented suitcase
stood at our front door
waiting for the train

that would take him
to a new house, a new wife,
a new family.
My mother

with a drowned handkerchief
lay face down on her bed
waving goodbye
to marriage.

I sat
in an attic room
bustling with departures
and people hugging each other

through jolting windows.
A solitary pigeon
perched on a high ledge
as the train pulled out.

Norman Silver

Two Dead Robins

In the driveway, their bodies so small
I almost stepped on them, two baby robins,
enormous mouths, bulging eyes, bodies thin wire
stretched over taut skin frames, bones showing
like aroused veins.
              It looked as though they'd either
tried to fly from the nest above
or the wind had swept them down. For some reason
I couldn't bear to pick them up in my hands,
so got a spade and buried them quickly
at the back of the garden, thinking as I did it

how many will die today, have much worse burial
than these two my shovel mixes under?

Raymond Souster

Lydia

People in the neighborhood were used to the evening
   breeze
bring Lydia's calling into their homes.
Everyone in the little town knew what would happen at
   the end of the day.
As soon as twilight came, crazy Lydia would sit on her
   decrepit
porch and call, for at least fifteen minutes,
'Isabel . . . Isabel . . . come here . . .'

No one heard the despair in her voice any longer.
No one felt pity any more.
Lydia had been crying her evening cries for so many
   years!
It had become as insignificant as the yapping of a
   farmyard dog.

Children and strangers would sometimes ask the
   meaning
of her calling.
Then the tale was told with words long drained of
   empathy.
They would explain that crazy Lydia had had a baby,
many years ago.
Just imagine, Lydia a baby!
The authorities, of course, decided that it could not be
   tolerated.
A civil servant and a nurse had placed the orange crate
   in which
Lydia had carefully tucked her little daughter on the
   back seat,
and had driven away.

The only thing to do, people said.
Nobody had ever told Lydia where the official car had
    gone.
And that was a good thing too, people said.

In this town lived many mothers who had a baby to
    cherish.
Lydia could only cry a name in the twilight.
For years.
And always in vain.
No one ever opened the gate to chat a bit.
Not until twenty years of pleading had passed.
On a fine summer's evening someone, out of the blue,
    joined
Lydia on the porch, said, 'Hello,' and filled his pipe.

Lydia did not answer his greeting; she didn't know how,
    for no one had ever greeted her before.
The man told her a short and simple tale.
But Lydia must have thought it a most wonderful story.
He said, 'Because of my work I got to know your
    daughter Isabel.
And now listen carefully, Lydia.
She always had enough to eat.
Always enough clothes.
And every night she slept in a warm bed with blankets.
Then she got sick one day. She had no pain, but lives no
    more.'
'That's nice,' said Lydia, as if she had received a gift.
'That's nice,' she said once more.
And she sat motionless on her porch.
As deeply peaceful as a person can be when a wall of
    loneliness
has been removed.

After that evening the little town said,
'Lydia is crazier than ever.
No, she doesn't cry any more, not that.
But do you know what she does now?
She waves at the clouds.
And laughs!'

Lize Stilma

(*trans. from the Dutch by Lous Heshusius
and Adrian Peetoom*)

He Treats them to Ice-cream

Every Sunday they went for a walk together.
He, she
and the three children.

One night
when she tried to stop him going
to his other woman,
he pulled out a flick-knife
from under the mattress.

They still go for a walk
every Sunday,
he, she and the three children.
He treats them to ice-cream and they all laugh.
She too.

Anna Swirszczynska

*(trans. from the Polish by Margaret Marshment
and Grazyra Baran)*

The Violin-maker

With his wire spectacles and shiny bald head
in a room full of canaries,
he was the most famous instrument-maker,
and my parents had asked him
to make me a violin.
I remember: I was a schoolgirl; I climbed
the narrow dovecot staircase
next to a basket on a rope, intended
for hauling up mail or newspapers.
Then I became a student, and still no violin –
there was still some detail, something to finish.
Today my daughter needs it,
but the violin-maker frowns:
'I won't be hurried
just because people happen to inherit
an obsession with playing an instrument.'

Grete Tartler

89

The Shelter

The old men built a shelter
Where they could sit and talk
And watch the Western S.M.T buses
Throbbing through towards Kilmarnock.
They made a good job.
It was trim and snug
Against the Ayrshire rain;
Adaptable too, when daylight faded,
and courting couples used the facilities.

'You'll not find me in there,'
My grandfather sneered.
'That's for men who're going to die.'
And he went out to see
A man about a dog.

I remember the day of his funeral
(Low grey clouds drizzle from Baidland).
As the hearse purred past the shelter
The old men stood straight,
Bonnets doffed, for a departed friend.

Geddes Thomson

Bus Stop

Waiting at the bus stop,
Good day,
Work,
Play,
Bus come,
Not mine.

What's that land pon my face,
Warm,
Wet,
Gooey,
Ahhh,
them spit at me.

Blood rise,
Blood boil,
From toe to heel,
through calf and thigh,
through belly,
through heart,
Arms and brain,
Blood burning red,
Anger flow,
Ah who spit at me so!!!

Bus move
And gone,
Look up,
Shiny glass,
No face to see,
Who hate me?
Who humiliate me?

All alone,
Anger have no place to go,
turn to tears,
and spill,
and flow.

Carmen Tunde

High Altitude Infatuation

You were
five and a half feet
above London.
I was 33,000
feet above Athens
or somewhere like that.
Five hundred
miles an hour,
ground speed.
Twenty minutes
behind time.
I was writing.
I was head down,
writing posture.
Your perfume
walked past me
in the aisle.
I looked up
and there was
your perfume
walking past me.

Steve Turner

My Father's Eye

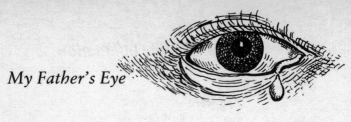

My father had a glass eye.

On Sundays when he stayed at home he would take other eyes out of his pocket, polish them with the edge of his sleeve and then call my mother to make her choice. My mother would giggle.

In the mornings my father was well satisfied. He would toss the eye in his hand before he wore it and would say it was a good eye. But I did not want to believe him.

I would throw a dark shawl over my shoulders as though I were cold but this was that I might spy on him. At least one day I saw him weeping. There was no difference at all from a real eye.

> *This poem*
> *Is not to be read*
> *By those who do not love me*
> *Not even*
> *By those*
> *Who will not know me*
> *If they do not believe I existed*
> *Like themselves*

After this episode with my father
I became suspicious even of those who had real eyes.

Eleni Vakalo

(trans. from the Greek by Kimon Friar)

94

threshold: toys or us

automatic double doors open:

> 'You carry the box,
> I'll carry the baby.'
> 'I'd rather carry the baby –
> he's lighter. *You* carry the box.'
> 'Fine –
> '– at least this one doesn't move around!'
> 'This one hugs!'

automatic double doors shut.

Evangelina Vigil-Piñón

Three Dollars Cash

Three dollars cash
For a pair of catalog shoes
Was what the midwife charged
My mama
For bringing me.
'We wasn't so country then,' says Mom,
'You being the last one –
And we couldn't, like
We done
When she brought your
Brother,
Send her out to the
Pen
and let her pick
Out
A pig.'

Alice Walker

Lonesome Walker

Walking drowsily, feeling dead,
Last night's music still playing in my head.
Foot-rhythm getting slower.
Yesterday's clothes clinging to me.
Backache from this morning's cardboard bed.
People staring at me, giving dirty looks.
Heavy traffic –
Car horns pumping into my head.
The pain from last night's comforts
Runs through me,
But I've got to keep on walking.
Ah, three girls!
Must look trim – look flash.
Start bouncing.
One hand in pocket – must look good . . .
They didn't even look.
They've got no taste – cho!
Feel drowsy.
Feel dead.
Must keep walking,
Walking,
Walking,
Walking to nowhere.

Denis Watson

Saturday night at Shaftesbury Avenue

The twenty-second of September
Ninteen hundred and ninety
Was a day I shall . . .
Forget.
I shall forget the brown polo-neck,
The milkshake, the ambience of that
claustrophobic bar.
I shall forget thin fingers, snooker cues
and your smile.
The slot-machine and Cinzano and ice.
I shall forget the puddles lying
Still and sensual on the pavement,
The way you splashed and threw
Your head back.
I shall forget,
Forget the way you brushed her hand,
As my throat grows tighter,
I shall forget.

Elizabeth Wells (16)

He who is never wrong

He hit me yesterday,
He who is never wrong
Hit me yesterday.
He thought I had borrowed his pen.
I hadn't.
I said, 'Have you looked under the bed?'
But he said that it would be
A ridiculous place
For me to hide his pen
And so he didn't look there.
It was there, I know.
I hid it,
Just to see if
He who is never wrong
Could be wrong.
He was.

Samantha West (14)

December

I'm driving down the Leeds ring road
it's seven o'clock at night
and starting to snow.

It's got to be doing sixty
as it flashes past
shiny black hearse flecked with snow
complete with coffin and wreaths.

Tail-lights flare
and then glow as he goes through
on amber
leaving me at the red
wondering
about the grieving family
around a torchlit grave
moving slowly from foot to foot
as a man in an overcoat
returns from the phone
and rejoins the group
with a shake of his head.

Martyn Wiley

Looking Out

It must be odd
to be a minority
he was saying.
I looked around
and didn't see any.
So I said
Yeah
it must be.

Mitsuye Yamada

The Night Before Goodbye*

Mama is mending
my underwear
while my brothers sleep.
Her husband taken away by the FBI
one son lured away by the Army
now another son and daughter
lusting for the free world outside.
She must let go.
The war goes on.
She will take one still small son
and join Papa in internment
to make a family.
Still sewing
squinting in the dim light
in room C barrack 4 block 4
she whispers
Remember
keep your underwear
in good repair
in case of accident
don't bring shame
on us.

Mitsuye Yamada

* Written about the time Japanese Americans were interned during the Second
World War

jumping into joy

reaching to light my cigarette your hand
trembles   i know you are
tired and not so well   but still a wave of
wanting swoops up my
belly
     it sticks
hard in the back of my throat
though   so i don't catch your
hand   i don't
run my hand down and over into your soft
palm   i don't shift
chairs to the empty one i've a moment of
caution barricaded myself with   i don't
run my fingers slow along your
arm or through your hair

in fact i don't
do anything but watch
you   self-conscious in dark
glasses   telling me this and
that about yourself
                    and i don't
know what's the
matter with me   i don't
want you to go   and i kiss
you goodbye just that fraction of a second
longer than i ought
to   for discretion
                    but i don't
turn and watch you
disappearing and i don't turn and

chase you up the road and catch your
arm and turn you to
face me   and i don't
say what i'm
thinking

back at
work   my knees
buckle   i'm just
jelly   but there's a
crisis   i have to
pull myself together   whip
myself into shape and get
on with it

            all afternoon
though and deep into the evening till i
drift into sleep   you keep
sweeping all over me and i can
see i'm in over my
head already and that it's deep
water
         but for
me   and i hope you
agree   it feels like
jumping into joy

Marg Yeo

Starting at Dawn

Under the waning moon
In the dawn –
A frosty bell.
My horse's hooves
Tramp through the yellow leaves.
As the sun rises
Not a human being is visible,
Only the sound of a stream
Through the misty trees.

Sun Yün-feng

(*trans. from the Chinese by Kenneth Rexroth
and Ling Chung*)

Before They Came

Before they came
roses sprouted on
my window-sill and blossomed.

the vines reached up
and made a thousand stairways green.

My house leaned and bathed
in the sun's rays

and I dreamt of bread
for all the people . . .

But that was before they came
with a blood-stained
tank

Tawfiq Zayyad

(*trans. from the Arabic by John Mikhail Asfour*)

When I had my operation
I displayed a lot of guts,
I could take it, smile, and like it,
But the bedpan drove me nuts.

                    Anon.

A letter was returned to the Post Office with the following inscription: 'Dead. Address unknown.'

Anon.

Acknowledgements

Acknowledgements

The editor and publishers gratefully acknowledge the following for permission to reproduce copyright poems in this book:

'Halfway Street, Sidcup' by Fleur Adcock from *The Incident Book*, published by Oxford University Press, 1986, copyright © Fleur Adcock, 1986, reprinted by permission of the publisher; 'Love at First Sight' by John Agard from *Lovelines for a Goat-born Lady*, published by Serpent's Tail, 1990, copyright © John Agard, 1990, reprinted by kind permission of John Agard c/o Caroline Sheldon Literary Agency; 'I had to get up early last Sunday' by Sandra Agard from *Talking Blues*, published by Centerprise, 1976, copyright © Sandra Agard, 1976, reprinted by permission of Centerprise Trust Ltd; 'Taking a Visitor to See the Ruins' by Paula Gunn Allen from *Wounds Beneath the Flesh*, published by White Pine Press, 1987, copyright © White Pine Press, 1987; 'Dad said' and 'I feel exhausted!' Anon. from *Kidstuff* by Roger Goff, published by ITV Books in association with Michael Joseph, 1982; 'Real Life' by Bob Arnold from *An Ear to the Ground*, published by The University of Georgia Press, 1987, copyright © Bob Arnold, 1987; 'seven' by Astra from *Back You Come Mother Dear* by Astra, published by Virago Press, 1986, copyright © Astra, 1986, reprinted by permission of the author; '13 and 625 Lines' by Ros Barber from *Hard Lines 3: New Poetry & Prose chosen by Ian Dury,*

Tom Paulin & Fanny Dubes, published by Faber & Faber Ltd, reprinted by permission of the publisher; 'Changing the Wheel' by Bertolt Brecht from *Poems 1913–1956 by Bertolt Brecht* translated by Michael Hamburger, published by Methuen London, 1976, copyright © Methuen London, 1976 and 1979, reprinted by permission of the publisher; 'Road' by Pete Brown from *Let 'em Roll Kafka*, published by Fulcrum Press; 'A Friend of the Indians' by Joseph Bruchac from *Wounds Beneath the Flesh*, published by White Pine Press, 1987, copyright © Joseph Bruchac, 1987, reprinted by permission of the publisher; 'education' and 'coffee' by Charles Bukowski from *You Get So Alone At Times That It Just Makes Sense*, published by Black Sparrow Press, copyright © Charles Bukowski, 1986, reprinted by permission of the publisher; 'The Day I Married . . .' by Jo Carson from *Stories I Ain't Told Nobody Yet*, published by Orchard Books, 1989; 'Picture from the Blitz' by Lois Clark from *Another Dimension*, published by Outposts Publications, 1982, copyright © Lois Clark, 1982; 'One night in 1940' by Dan Colman from *I Never Saw My Father Nude*, published by Arthur Barker, 1981, copyright © Dan Colman, 1981, reprinted by permission of Weidenfeld & Nicholson; 'A Recollection' by Frances Cornford from *Collected Poems*, published by Hutchinson, 1954, copyright © the Estate of Frances Cornford, 1954, reprinted by permission of Random House UK Ltd; 'right here the other night something' by e.e. cummings from *73 poems by e.e. cummings*, published by Faber & Faber Ltd; 'Fire Down Below' by Ginnie Lewis Digham from *Poems From Hengoed Low Level*, published by Tiger Bay Press, 1987, copyright © Tiger Bay Press & Ginnie Lewis Digham, 1987; 'Sexism in 1972' by Jas H. Duke from *Off the Record* compiled by PI O, published by Penguin Books

Australia, reprinted by permission of the publisher; 'Happy Mothers Day' by Sharon Dunham from *Sub Animal Yells*, published by Centerprise, 1984, copyright © Sharon Dunham, 1984, reprinted by permission of Centerprise Trust Ltd; 'I nearly died' by Bill Eburn from *Rising Tide*, published by London Voices; 'The Trust' by Saqi Farooqi from *A Listening Game* published by Lokamaya Press, 1987, copyright © Saqi Farooqi, translation copyright © Lokamaya Press, 1987; 'Programme cover' by Evelyne Freeman from *Cadbury's Ninth Book of Children's Poetry*, published by Red Fox, 1991, copyright © The National Exhibition of Children's Art, 1991, reprinted by permission of The National Exhibition of Children's Art; 'Four Years' by Pamela Gillilan from *That Winter*, published by Bloodaxe Books, 1986, copyright © Pamela Gillilan, 1986, reprinted by permission of the publisher; 'Family Matters' by Günter Grass from *Selected Poems* translated by Michael Hamburger, published by Martin Secker & Warburg Ltd, 1966, copyright © Martin Secker & Warburg Ltd, 1966, reprinted by permission of the publisher; 'Just Waiting' by Monique Griffiths from *Times Like These*, published by Obatala Press, 1988; 'Tribal Cemetery' by Janet Campbell Hale from *New and Old Voices of Wah' Kon-Tah*, published by International Publishers, New York; 'Well, it's Today Already' by Martin Hall from *Comic Verse* edited by Roger McGough, published by Kingfisher Books, copyright © Grisewood and Dempsey, 19**, reprinted by permission of the publisher; 'Feet' by Mark Haviland, published by Thap Publishing, reprinted by permission of the author; 'Morning Poem' by Adrian Henri from *Collected Poems*, published by Jonathan Cape Ltd, reprinted by permission of Rogers, Coleridge & White Ltd; 'The Steam Car' by Miroslav Holub from *Vanishing Lung*

Syndrome, published by Faber & Faber Ltd, reprinted by permission of the publisher; 'A War Film' by Teresa Hooley from *Songs For All Seasons*, published by Jonathan Cape Ltd, 1927, copyright © The Estate of the late Teresa Hooley, 1927, reprinted by permission of the publisher and the author's estate; 'The Changing Face of an Actress' by Michael Horovitz from *Growing Up: Selected Poems and Pictures 1951–79*, published by Allison & Busby, 1979, copyright © Michael Horowitz, 1979, reprinted by permission of the author; 'Pants For True' by Gloria T. Hull from *Healing Heart*, published by Kitchen Table: Women of Color Press Inc., USA, 1989, copyright © Gloria T. Hull, 1989, reprinted by permission of the publisher; 'The Australian Mongrel' by Jeltje from *Off The Record* compiled by PI O, published by Penguin Books Australia Ltd, reprinted by permission of the publisher; 'The guy' by Jenny Kentish from *Take a Chance*, published by The Australian Association for the Teaching of English, 1981, copyright © Jenny Kentish, 1981, reprinted by permission of the publisher; 'I never got what I wanted' by R.D. Laing from *Knots*, published by Tavistock Publications, 1970, copyright © The R.D. Laing Trust, 1970, reprinted by permission of Routledge; 'Parents' by Julius Lester from *Search for the New Land*; 'Roman Holiday' by Tony Lewis-Jones from *Down To Earth and On Its Feet*, published by Bristol Broadsides Ltd, 1987, copyright © Tony Lewis-Jones & Alana Farrell, 1987, reprinted by permission of the publisher; 'Daniel at Breakfast' by Phyllis McGinley from *The Love Letters of Phyllis McGinley*, published by Viking Penguin, a division of Penguin Books USA Inc., 1954, copyright © Phyllis McGinley, 1954, copyright renewed © Phyllis Hayden Blake, 1982, reprinted by permission of the publisher; 'Overheard in a hospital examination cubicle' by

J.M. McKenzie from *The Quote Unquote Book of Eaves-droppings* edited by Nigel Rees, published by Unwin Paperbacks, copyright © Peters, Fraser & Dunlop, reprinted by permission of the Peters, Fraser & Dunlop Group Ltd; 'True Life Romance' by Lindsay MacRae from *Dancing the Tightrope*, published by The Women's Press, 1987, copyright © Lindsay MacRae, 1987, reprinted by permission of the author; 'I went to my uncles wedding' by Mario from *Vote for Love* compiled by Nanette Newman, published by Collins, 1976, copyright © Brian Forbes Ltd; 'Classroom' by Tania Mead from *A Book to Write Poems By*, published by The Australian Association for the Teaching of English, 1983, copyright © Tania Mead, 1983, reprinted by permission of the publisher; 'Wednesday Chronicle' by Pamela Mordecai from *New Poets From Jamaica: An Anthology*, published by Savacou Publications Ltd, 1979, copyright © Savacou Publications, 1979; 'My lover capable of terrible lies' by Kaccipēṭṭu Naṉṉākaiyār from *The Interior Landscape: Love Poems From a Classical Tamil Anthology* translated by A. K. Ramanujan, published by Indiana University Press, British copyright © Peter Owen Ltd, reprinted by permission of Peter Owen Ltd; 'Alcazar' by John Newlove from *The Fat Man*, published by McClelland & Stewart Inc., Canada, copyright © John Newlove, reprinted by permission of the publisher; 'Varicose Story' by Caterina Passoni from *Off the Record* compiled by PI O, published by Penguin Books Australia Ltd, reprinted by permission of the publisher; 'Unemployed' by Piedro Pietri from *Puerto Rican Obituary*, published by Monthly Review Press, 1973, copyright © Piedro Pietri, 1973; 'Drag Act' by Fiona Pitt-Kethley from *The Perfect Man*, published by Sphere Books Ltd, copyright © Fiona Pitt-Kethley, reprinted by permission of Sheil Land Associates; 'Pain' by Shamsur Rahman from *Poems From Bangladesh: The Voice of a New Nation* translated by Pritish Nandy, published by The Lyrebird Press Ltd, 1972, copyright © Pritish Nandy, 1972; 'To the Heart' by Tadeusz Różewicz from *Postwar Polish Poetry* by Czeslaw Milosz, published by Doubleday, 1965, translation copyright © Czeslaw Milosz, 1965, reprinted by permission of Doubleday, a division of Bantam Doubleday Dell Publishing Group, Inc.; 'I don't believe this' by E. Russell from *Grass Roots in Verse* ed. Arif Ali & Catherine Hogben, published by Hansib Publishing Ltd, 1988, copyright © Hansib Publishing Ltd, 1988; 'Implications' by Carl Sandburg from *Good Morning, America*, published by Harcourt Brace Jovanovich, Inc., copyright © Carl Sandburg, 1928 and renewed 1956, reprinted by permission of the publisher; 'They Carried Their Truth to the Ditch Where They Were Thrown' by Christian Santos from *Amar Go: Central American Women's Poetry For Peace* translated by Anna Kirwan Vogel & Isabella Halstead, published by Granite Press, 1987, copyright © Christian Santos, 1987; 'Decorated' by Siegfried Sassoon from *The War Poems of Siegfried Sassoon*, published by Faber & Faber Ltd, copyright © The Estate of Siegfried Sassoon; 'The Cashmere Shawl' by Jaroslav Seifert from *Selected Poems*, published by André Deutsch Ltd, reprinted by permission of the publisher; 'The Pigeon' by Norman Silver from *Words on a Faded T-shirt* by Norman Silver, published by Faber & Faber Ltd, reprinted by permission of the publisher; 'Two Dead Robins' by Raymond Souster from *The Collected Poems of Raymond Souster*, published by Oberon Press, Canada, n/a, copyright © Raymond Souster, n/a, reprinted by permission of Oberon Press; 'Lydia' by Lize Stilma from *Portraits*, published by Mosaic Press, Canada, 1986, translated by Lous Heshusius and Adrian Peetoom, copyright © Lous Heshusius and Adrian Peetoom, 1986, original Dutch copyright © Uitgeverij INTRO, 1985, reprinted by permission of Mosaic Press; 'He Treats them to Ice-cream' by Anna Swirszczynska from *Fat Like the Sun* translated by Margaret Marshment and Grazyna Baran, 1986, published by The Women's Press, 1986, copyright © Anna Swirszczynska's Estate, 1980, translation copyright © Margaret Marshment and Grazyna Baran, reprinted by permission of the translators; 'The Violin-maker' by Grete Tartler from *Orient Express* translated by Fleur Adcock, published by Oxford University Press, 1989, copyright © Fleur Adcock, 1989, reprinted by permission of the publisher; 'The Shelter' by Geddes Thomson, published by Voices; 'Bus Stop' by Carmen Tunde from *Black Women Talk Poetry*, published by Black Womantalk Ltd, 1987, copyright © Black Womantalk, 1987, reprinted by permission of the author; 'High Altitude Infatuation' by Steve Turner from *Up to Date*, published by Hodder & Stoughton Ltd, reprinted by permission of the publisher; 'My Father's Eye' by Eleni Vakalo from *A Book of Women Poets From Antiquity To Now* translated by Kimon Friar, edited by Aliki Barnstone & Willis Barnstone, published by Schocken Books, New York, copyright © Eleni Vakalo & Kimon Friar; 'threshold: toys or us' by Evangelina Vigil-Piñón from *The Computer is Down*, published by Arte Publico Press, 1987, copyright © Evangelina Vigil-Piñón, 1987, reprinted by permission of the publisher; 'Three Dollars Cash' by Alice Walker from *Revolutionary Petunias*, published by The Women's Press, reprinted by permission of David Higham Associates; 'Lonesome Walker' by Denis Watson from *Bluefoot Traveller* edited by James Berry; 'Saturday night at Shaftesbury Avenue' by Elizabeth Wells from *Cadbury's Ninth Book of Children's Poetry*, published by Red Fox, 1991, copyright © The National Exhibition of Children's Art, 1991, reprinted by permission of The National Exhibition of Children's Art; 'He who is never wrong' by Samantha West from *Cadbury's Eighth Book of Children's Poetry*, published by Red Fox, 1991, copyright © The National Exhibition of Children's Art, 1991, reprinted by permission of The National Exhibition of Children's Art; 'December' by Martyn Wiley from *The Live Album*, published by Stride, 1988, copyright © Martyn Wiley, 1988; 'Looking Out' and 'The Night Before Goodbye' by Mitsuye Yamada from *Camp Notes & Other Poems*, published by Shameless Hussey Press, 1976, copyright © Mitsuye Yamada, 1976, reprinted by permission of the author; 'jumping into joy' by Marg Yeo from *Dancing the Tightrope*, published by The Women's Press, 1987, copyright © Marg Yeo, 1987; 'Starting at Dawn' by Sun Yün-feng from *Kenneth Rexroth: Women Poets of China*, published by New Directions Publishing Corp., 1972, copyright © Kenneth Rexroth, 1972, reprinted by permission of the publisher; 'Before They Came' from 'Six Words' by Tawfiq Zayyad from *When the Words Burn: An Anthology of Modern Arabic Poetry* translated by John Mikhail Asfour, published by Cormorant Books, Canada, 1988, copyright © John Mikhail Asfour, 1988, reprinted by permission of John Mikhail Asfour; 'When I had my operation' Anon. from *Sweet and Sour*, edited by Christopher Logue, published by B. T. Batsford Ltd, 1983, copyright © Christopher Logue, reprinted by permission of the publisher; 'A letter was returned to the Post Office' Anon. from *More Things I Wish I'd Said, and Some I Wish I Hadn't*, collected by Kenneth Edwards, published by Abelard, copyright © Blackie Books, reprinted by permission of Blackie Books.

Every effort has been made to trace copyright holders, but in a few cases this has proved impossible. The editor and publishers apologize for these cases of unwilling copyright transgression and would like to hear from any copyright holders not acknowledged.

Index of First Lines

Index of First Lines

Also in Puffin

ALEX

Tessa Duder

In a few minutes I will dive into that water waiting at my feet. A minute later I'll either be ecstatic or a failure.

It is 1959, and Alex is swimming to qualify for the Olympic Games in Rome. In the past year she has fallen in love and has known what it is to lose – in swimming and in life. Now she must swim the race of her life.

FEET AND OTHER STORIES

Jan Mark

Nobody looks at feet.

But after being spurned by the school's tennis hero, Jane does look at feet, and makes a surprising discovery.